FRESH
Flowers FOR
YOU
DAUGHTER

COUNTRYMAN

www.jcountryman.com
A division of Thomas Nelson, Inc.
www.thomasnelson.com

Copyright © 2002 by J. Countryman,
a division of Thomas Nelson, Inc., Nashville, Tennessee 37214

Compiled and edited by Terri Gibbs.

All rights reserved. No portion of this publication may be
reproduced, stored in a retrieval system or transmitted in any
form by any means—electronic, mechanical, photocopying,
recording, or any other—except for brief quotations in printed
reviews, without the prior written permission of the publisher.

Designed by Garborg Design Works, Minneapolis, Minnesota

Photos by Lisa Garborg

www.thomasnelson.com

ISBN: 08499-9600-7

Printed and bound in USA.

You are brighter than apples,
Sweeter than tulips,
You are the great flood of our souls.

AMY LOWELL

When a girl is
born, it's a success
for the family.

YIDDISH PROVERB

*To have you in our family
makes us a success. Not only
have you made us a successful
family . . . you've made us a
happy family.*

A baby is an inestimable
blessing and bother.

MARK TWAIN

How happy
for me that
you happened
to be far more
blessing than
bother.

You have always been one of God's greatest gifts to me.

A daughter is
a gift whose
worth cannot
be measured
except by
the heart.

ANONYMOUS

A thing of beauty is a joy forever.

JOHN KEATS

The beauty of your life
will forever be
a joy to me.

Real confidence comes from knowing and accepting yourself—your strengths and your limitations.

JUDITH BARDWICK

You have more potential than you realize—and enough humility to keep you striving for the best.

May all the bounty you give
away come back doubly
blessed to you.

Those who give

cheerfully give

twice—once to

others, once

to themselves.

ANONYMOUS

Love is that condition in which
the happiness of another person
is essential to your own.

ROBERT A. HEINLEIN

I guess that's why loving you
makes me so happy!
I want God's best for you,
in every area of life.

The world is a pretty
good sort of a world,
and it is our duty to
make the best of it,
and be thankful.

BENJAMIN FRANKLIN

*Make the most of all
you've been given. You are
Queen of all you've got.*

May you always find the
joy that comes from
reaching a little higher,
doing things a little better.

Originality consists not only in

doing things differently, but

also in "doing things better."

EDWARD STEDMAN

False notes at a concert are only human. Why does everything have to be perfect?

VLADIMIR HOROWITZ

You may not be perfect, but you're perfectly adorable to me.

It is only with the
heart that one
can see rightly.

ANTOINE DE
SAINT EXUPERY

*I see in you potential for great
and noble things, because you
have a great and noble heart.*

Not I, nor anyone else can
travel that road for you, you
must travel it for yourself.

WALT WHITMAN

If I could I would suffer all
the pain and disappointment
of life for you. But that
would be cheating you of
life in all its fullness.

May God grant you the wisdom to walk where He leads, to follow His footsteps.

Wisdom
is knowing
what to
do next;
virtue is
doing it.

DAVID
JORDAN

The seat of knowledge
is in the head;
wisdom in the heart.

WILLIAM HAZLITT

The wise woman will
purpose to pursue both
knowledge and wisdom.
She combines the best of
what she knows with the
depth of what she feels.

Give love, and love to your life will flow,

A strength in your utmost need;

Have faith, and a score of hearts will show

Their faith in your work and deed.

MARY AINGE DE VERE

Just as the ripe fruit breaks off from the tree, so a time will come when you will have to break off from your mother.

ISOKO HATANO

I'm so glad for the day you became more than my daughter—you became my friend.

I want you to live in the best place you can afford, eat well, and if there is anything left, send some to Mama.

PEARL BAILEY

Well . . . I do want you to live well and eat well.

In your life I see so many of the things I hoped and wished for . . . and so many wonderful things I hardly dared dream for!

A child's character is like good soup. Both are homemade.

ANONYMOUS

Each child
carries his
own blessing
into the world.

YIDDISH
PROVERB

God went overboard
with blessings when
He gave you to me.

Look life straight in the eye, and don't be afraid to ask "why."

The simplest achievements of life, as well as the bigger ones take—a little nerve.

MARJORIE HOLMES

When the path of life becomes difficult and discouraging, keep your feet steady on the way to the goal in front of you, and you will do just fine.

All rising to a great place
is by a winding stair.

FRANCIS BACON

Your charming, caring
heart will always be
filled with beauty.

A beauty is a woman you notice;

a charmer is one who notices you.

ADLAI E. STEVENSON

We are happy
in this world just
in proportion
as we make
others happy.

JOSH BILLINGS

Like the glow of a rose,
your life is a bright
spot of kindness and
concern for others.

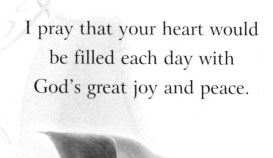

I pray that your heart would
be filled each day with
God's great joy and peace.

Joy is not
in things;
it is in us.

RICHARD
WAGNER

The hand that rocks the cradle
may not rule the world, but it
certainly makes it a better place.

MARGERY HURST

Daughters like you
make rocking the cradle,
so very worthwhile.

People who love
each other fully
and truly are the
happiest people
in the world.

MOTHER TERESA

Loving you has been one of the
most fulfilling joys of my life.
You've been better than a meadow
full of four-leaf clover.

Pages and pages of prose
could only begin to tell the
world how proud I am of you.

The tongue is the
pen of the heart.

YIDDISH PROVERB

*I'll be the first to admit I
was never a perfect mother,
but somehow my perfectly
wonderful daughter made up
for all my imperfections.*

You have a child,
and you can't be a
perfectionist anymore.

MARY BETH HURT

God's tenderness in the springing grass,

His beauty in the flowers,

His living love in the sun above—

All here, and near, and ours!

GILMAN

My heart rejoices at your joy,
Weeps at your sorrow,
Smiles at your delight,
And hopes for your tomorrow.

It's not flesh and
blood . . . but
hearts that make
us mother and
daughter.

ANONYMOUS

One's own

is beloved.

YIDDISH
PROVERB

You are beloved every moment,
special girl of my dreams come true.

Have the courage to
face the future with
fortitude—and a fling!

Courage is the ladder
on which all the other
virtues mount

CLARE BOOTHE LUCE

You have every reason
in the world to walk
tall. I'm so proud to
call you my daughter.

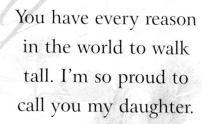

Never bend your
head! Always
hold it high! Look
the world straight
in the eye!

HELEN KELLER

Children are
the anchors
that hold a
mother to life.

SOPHOCLES

*You have certainly been
an anchor for me in the
deep, stormy sea of life.*

How I've enjoyed the love
and laughter of life with a
daughter like you!

An atmosphere of truth, love,
and humor can nourish
extraordinary human capacity.

MARILYN FERGUSON

When a woman hears her baby's first cry, or holds it for the first time in her arms, she knows that she has been party to a miracle.

MARJORIE HOLMES

A mother is a person who seeing there are only four pieces of pie for five people, promptly announces she never did care for pie.

TENNEVA JORDAN

I hope you understand the depth of my love for you. I hope you have seen that all these growing-up years. (So often we were both growing up.)

Be of good courage, and He
shall strengthen your heart.

PSALM 30:24

May God in His unending
goodness fill your spirit
with His love and power.

What are these drops of oil in our lamps? They are the little things of everyday life: fidelity, little words of kindness, just a little thought for others.

MOTHER TERESA

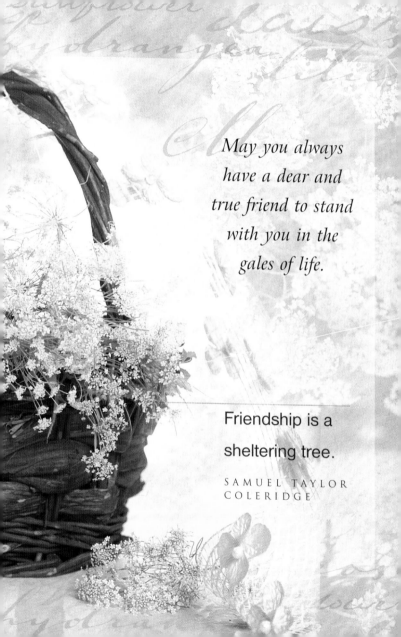

May you always have a dear and true friend to stand with you in the gales of life.

Friendship is a sheltering tree.

SAMUEL TAYLOR
COLERIDGE

There are no ideal mothers,
nor are there ideal daughters.

PHYLLIS MAGRAB

Life would probably be
pretty boring if there were.

Remember, your heavenly
Father is only a prayer away.

To the one who strives earnestly,
God also lends a helping hand.

AESCHYLUS

Do what
you judge to
be beautiful and
honest, though
you acquire no
glory from it.

PYTHAGORAS

*I admire the way you care
for others, even when no
one knows or notices. You
are an inspiration to me.*

*In gazing at your face I
see not only my daughter
but a unique woman.*

In thy face I see
the map of honor,
truth, and loyalty.

SHAKESPEARE

No bird soars too
high, if he soars
with his wings.

WILLIAM BLAKE

Soar as high as you can.
And when you can soar no higher,
let God be your support.

I am confident you will be
an incomparable mother to
my grandchildren, should
God give them to me.

A mother is not to
be compared with
another person—she
is incomparable.

AFRICAN PROVERB

Hold fast your dreams!

Within you heart

Keep one still, secret spot

Where dreams may go,

And, sheltered so,

May thrive and grow

Where doubt and fear are not.

LOUISE DRISCOLL

May you live to the
fullest all the great and
wonderful things God
has planned for you.

Having a purpose in life, throw into

your work such strength of mind

and muscle as God has given you.

CARLYLE

*Is it any wonder that a day
with you is always a happy,
friendly sort of day?*

There are those
who have the gift
of finding joy
everywhere and
of leaving it
behind them
when they go.

FABER

A wise bee knows
the sweetest
honey is made
from bitter flowers.

FOLK WISDOM

I would protect you from life's
pain and sorrow if I could,
but that wouldn't be good
for you... or for me.

To a mother,
children are
like ideas;
none are as
wonderful
as her own.

CHINESE
PROVERB

There will never
be anyone as
sweet and
special as you.
And that's a
wonderful idea!

How happy the
heart that
shines with
love like yours.

Your smile is

a light in the

window of

your face.

ANONYMOUS

*Sometimes I forget to tell
you how proud I am of the
woman you have become.
You are very special to me.*

It is not what she has,

or even what she does

that directly expresses

the worth of a woman,

but what she is.

AMIEL

We cannot live
pleasantly
without living
wisely and
nobly and
righteously.

E P I C U R U S

I pray that your heart
would always be tender to
the truth of God's love.

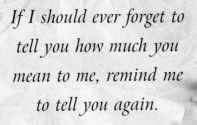

If I should ever forget to
tell you how much you
mean to me, remind me
to tell you again.

I like not only to be loved, but

to be told that I am loved.

GEORGE ELIOT

A loving heart
is the truest
wisdom.

DICKENS

As you reach out to love
and care for others your
heart will gain wisdom, and
your love will grow deeper.

A mother is she who can take the
place of all others but whose
place none can take.

CARDINAL MERMILLOD

God's goodness has been
great to thee;
Let never day nor night
unhallowed pass,
But still remember what the
Lord has done.

SHAKESPEARE

It is when tomorrow's
burden is added to the
burden of today, that
the weight is more
than we can bear.

MACDONALD

Walk one day at a time with God.
He will take care of tomorrow.

Nothing is so strong as
gentleness, nothing is so
gentle as real strength.

DE SALES

Through life may you find the
perfect balance between womanly
strength and gentleness—strength
and support, gentleness and grace.

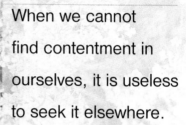

When we cannot
find contentment in
ourselves, it is useless
to seek it elsewhere.

LA ROCHEFOUCAULD

Be content to be the person
God wants you to be.
Striving for sophistication
and worldly pleasures is silly.

May God use your talents to reach out to a world that needs all you have to give.

Love of truth
shows itself
in this, that
a [woman]
knows how to
find and value
the good in
everything.

GOETHE

To love is to find pleasure in the
happiness of the person loved.

LEIBNITZ

To love and care for you these
many years has brought me more
happiness than I can describe.

The LORD bless you and
keep you;
The LORD make His face
shine upon you
And be gracious to you;
The LORD lift up His
countenance upon you,
And give you peace.

NUMBERS 6:24-26

A perplexing and ticklish
possession is a daughter.

THOMAS HARDY

Perplexing? Yes!
Frustrating? At times.
Exasperating? Definitely.
But oh so wonderful,
most of the time!

The amicable loosening of the bond between daughter and mother is one of the most difficult tasks of education.

ALICE BALINT

When I see your little bark slipping
out of the bay,
I bow my head and pray,
"Go with my girl, dear God, today."

Say the word "daughter" slowly, prolong its gentle sound. Notice the way it lingers on the tongue like a piece of candy.

PAUL ENGLE

I'm blessed to be a member of that privileged club: Mothers of Daughters.

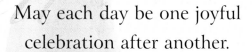

May each day be one joyful
celebration after another.

Nothing is
more highly to
be prized than
the value of
each day.

GOETHE

If you wish to be loved, love.

SENECA

As you give, you will receive,
blessings and bounty and
love for a lifetime.

Life must be measured by thought and action, not by time.

LUBBOCK

No one can do everything,
but everyone can do something.
What you do, depends on you.

When you smile…
the birds sing,
the flowers bloom,
and my heart sings too.

What sunshine is to flowers,
smiles are to humankind. They
are but trifles, to be sure, but
scattered along life's pathway, the
good they do is inconceivable.

ADDISON

A good [woman] is
the best friend, and
therefore soonest to
be chosen, longer
to be retained; and
indeed, never to
be parted with.

TAYLOR

Friends are like flowers. You
can never have too many.

Pursue some path, however narrow and crooked, in which you can walk with love and reverence.

HENRY DAVID THOREAU

I'm cheering for you on your path. The one that means so much to you.

May the God of hope fill
you with all joy and peace.

ROMANS 15:13

This is my
prayer for you
daughter, each
and every day
of the year.

God's finger can
touch nothing but to
mold it into loveliness.

GEORGE MACDONALD

That's why I've known
all along that His finger
has touched you.